Arjun Singh

Social and religious significance of baolis in Jammu region

A retrospective preview

GRIN Publishing

Bibliographic information published by the German National Library:

The German National Library lists this publication in the National Bibliography; detailed bibliographic data are available on the Internet at http://dnb.dnb.de .

Imprint:

Copyright © 2014 GRIN Verlag GmbH
Print and binding: Books on Demand GmbH, Norderstedt Germany
ISBN: 978-3-656-86008-2

This book at GRIN:

http://www.grin.com/en/e-book/284489/social-and-religious-significance-of-baolis-in-jammu-region

GRIN - Your knowledge has value

Since its foundation in 1998, GRIN has specialized in publishing academic texts by students, college teachers and other academics as e-book and printed book. The website www.grin.com is an ideal platform for presenting term papers, final papers, scientific essays, dissertations and specialist books.

Visit us on the internet:

http://www.grin.com/

http://www.facebook.com/grincom

http://www.twitter.com/grin_com

SOCIAL AND RELIGIOUS SIGNIFICANCE OF BAOLIS IN JAMMU REGION: A RETROSPECTIVE PREVIEW.

Dr. Arjun Singh.

Assistant Professor, Chanderprabhu Jain College of Higher Studies & School of Law, Narella.(Affiliated to Guru Govind Singh Indraprastha University, Delhi)

Introduction

Heritage is a wide conception that encompasses our natural, indigenous and historic or cultural inheritance. It refers to something, which is inherited from one's ancestors something immaterial, as a style of philosophy that is passed from one generation to another. It can be divided into various categories but here we are concerned with the built heritage. Built heritage, in its broadest sense consists of an individual or group of buildings, structures, monuments, or installation or remains, which are associated with architectural, cultural, social, political, economic, or military history.

The *baolis* or natural water springs of Jammu region are unique examples where ecological and environment considerations have led to sanctifying of perennial water sources since ancient times. In grained into of the life of rhythm of hill and high land communities of outer Himalayan ranges of Jammu regions.[1] These sacred springs have evolved as cultural institutions that not only showcase social, religious practices but also are windows to native art and architecture[2].

Baolis or natural water springs constructed by the people form a special feature of hilly terrain. They not only serve as the natural sources of drinking water to the surrounding society but also became a means of expression of their religious devotion and concern for human welfare. In foothills from Basoli in the east to Rajouri and Punch in the west, *baolis* are found on roads and pathways. Natural spring and deep circular well tpes of bolis are common in the Jammu region. Only small number bears icons or sculptured slabs and friezes[3]. Most of these *baolis* are natural springs jutting out from the hillside with small recesses or alcoves to cover them and stepped basins to hold the water. Sometimes the walls of these alcoves are covered with sculptures in low relief displaying very crude workmanship indicative of the low ebb, which Hindu plastic art had reached in these in later centuries[4].

However, some panels in *baolis* in Basoli-Udhampur region are worked by superior workmanship in high relief. In Naushera-Rajouri region, most of the *baolis* existing from ancient times are devoid of sculptures in relief or icons.

But in recent years, the onset modern way of life has led to neglect of these natural water sources. Due to ready availability of tube well water through pipe lines in the rural homes, many of springs have either fall in ill disuse or begin allowed to fill up. This has endangered traditional institutions of natural water harvesting in Jammu region. Give way to lower most Himalayan ranges- the Shivalik outcrops- popularly called as Kandi belt. Full of thorny bushes, boulders, marked by narrow gorges and small valleys created by seasonal nullahs, this area of Duggar is most inhospitable terrain and is locally called as, "*Maro kandi*" – the deadly kandi. Arid and dry there is great shortage of water in these area.

Baolis in Jammu Shivaliks fall in two categories[5]. The small and most commonly found variety is simply called as "*Baoli*" or "*Baan*". Its size varies from 2 ft. to 10 ft. square reservoir with varying depth. A large spring with the considerable discharge is called as "*Naun*". Such springs, which are not frequently, encountered are large in size and measured between 10 to 15 ft. sq. and sometimes even more. Those some covered *baolies* are said to have been constructed in remote areas, but in the extent examples, a *baoli* as a matter of rule is an open- air structure. The point where underground water gushes out is converted into a reservoir or basin, built by stones bricks. Wide at the top and narrowing like a pond towards the base, these reservoirs look like inverted hallowed pyramids. Other than the most commonly found square variety, the springs are also seen in hexagonal and octagonal shapes.

Baolies are everywhere-in and around villages, on waysides, on foot routes in the Jammu region. Mostly being the only drinking water source for the local communities and the cattle, a spring located in the middle or near a village, is invariably the heart of the community. Males and females, old and young-gather to bathe, wash, offer worship to the gods, ancestors, heroes, sculpted on its walls, stop for a halt, exchange news and views, welcome outsiders and visitors, or simply be there and enjoy the cool environs, the murmur of quite flow or gurgle of gushing water and water falling from a spout. Attracting once in a day, almost every living and able bodies soul of the village- be it human, animal or bird- a *baoli* often acts as a village '*Chopal*'.

Being the perennial sources of life, the springs have acquired a semi-religious character during the course of time. Whenever a new spring was encased with masonry, it enclosing three walls decorated with 'sculptural relief's' of gods and goddesses and often a small Shiva temple standing in one of its one side elevate these springs from a plain source of water to a sacred place. Supporting a canopy on four pillars, these *Shivalayas* which are called as '*Chowkhandis*' along with images divine images on walls elevate *baolies* of Shivaliks as open-air shrines. Here natives after morning ablutions also offer worship respective gods and return home after completing morning's routine of a devout[6]. Many a times a spring is also the place to perform religious ceremonies as well as eschatological (after death) rituals. At the baolies in the premises of ancient group of temples at Devak, Purmandal, Jandrah, or Airma, natives from near as well as far off villages come to these places to perform last rites of their relatives.

In case an icon of a local *devta* is installed by the side of a spring, then the site becomes a place of '*meil*'-annual community gathering, of all those who worship that particular '*devta*'. The installation of the image of *Kouri Devta*, deity has made the group of springs as a place for annual fair. When the springs are located in the premises of pilgrimage center like Purmandal, Airwan, Devak, Jandrah, they acquire a special significance places as inseparable adjuncts to the holy place. Every pilgrim begins his or her visit by taking the ritual bath in the spring situated in the premises.

Existing alongside organized religious organizations like the one centered on a Hindu temple and as testified from the magnificent monuments of early mediaeval temples like Kiramchi, Babor and Billawar in Jammu region, *baolies* are very important historical and art historical institutions. The images sculpted on the *baoli* reliefs, not only reflect on the development of religious beliefs that held sway in Jammu region from time to time but also the development of different architectural styles as seen in the niches and pillars which enclose the main images. There also reference to contemporary fashions in dress, ornaments, weapons and other ethnographical details[7].

Baolies of Jammu region, therefore hold a special significance, especially when the history and culture of the region still has some unexplained areas for want of historical, religious, and artistic material evidences. The existing springs still attract number of natives but their number is decreasing day by day. Village *Panchyat* is the main caretaker of these *baolis* in the present time. Some of the important *baolis* of the Jammu region are:

SUMMARY AND DISCUSSION

1. Papa-Nashini baoli at Suddh Mahadev.

The best specimens of *baolis* sculptures are at the spring called *Papa-Nashini* at Suddh Mahadev[8] built during the eighteenth century, although the shrine said to have been constructed in early centuries. The cistern from which water flows out is Simha-Mukh stone water-duck. A number of sculptured panels have been embedded in its extensive stone walls. One of the panels beautifully depicts the *bhogasayana murti* of Vishnu. The figure of Vishnu lies on the coils of *Adisesha*, but because of paucity of space, it has been carved half reclining, while nine-hooded primeval serpent provides an umbrella-like covering. The four faces *Brahama* is shown seated on the long stalked lotus, which issues from the naval of Vishnu. The figure of *Lakshmi,* who is pressing his feet, is well formed with fully developed breasts. There may be some other deities filling gaps, like those of five *Ayudha-purusha.* Garuda and the demon *Madhu Kaitabha* which scriptures ordain to be made in such an icon. However, the icon is worn out; nothing else can be deciphered[9].

2. Dhan baoli.

The *baoli* of Dhan is the best preserved and contains sculptures of fine quality representative of sculptures of this class and a model of *baoli* art in Jammu region. This large *baoli* is situated at the foot of the descent into the khad about five kilometers from Thara-Kadwal and on way to Khun village. Its walls bear a number of remarkably well sculptured panels. The *baolis* and its sculptures may be assigned to a recent date. The basin is fifteen feet squares and of the usual type. Water gushes out of hillside through the mouth of a well-carved stone head of a lion. The *baoli* has a figure of *Ganesha* in it and other that of a coiled snake. The upper most terrace of the back wall of *baoli* contains three big takchas(alcoves) and two smaller ones. Of the bigger alcoves contains a figure of four-headed Brahma on a raised seat, with legs crossed and hands holding Vedas. All the heads are crowned and each face has a flowing beard. He is dressed in dhoti wears a rosary and a *Janeu.* The takcha in the middle contains figure of Siva and Parvati in high relief. They are seated on throne. Siva has a somewhat fat belly and his locks are done in a knot on his crown. Ganga flows from his hair. There are a snake entwined round his neck with its hood raised above his hair. A crescent moon is balanced above his third eye. He holds a trisul and a rosary in his right hand, a damru, and a circular object in his left. Both Siva and Parvati wear a bracelet. The foreparts of a bull and lion, their respective vahanas appear on their sides. The third niche contains Vishnu and Lakshmi. The crowned, four-armed Vishnu carries his usual ayudhas, gada (mace) sankh (conch) dises and padma (lotus) in his hands, Lakshmi sits on his left knee with folded hands, with end of sari drawn over her head[10].

3.The baoli of Lahdi.

The *baoli* of Ladhi situated about three miles away from Khun on way to Mansar Lake, has two terraced walls. The face of the lower wall is embellished with a course of rosettes, above which is another row of inverted flowers. The upper walls more ornamented. The front pilasters have their lower haves filled, the fillets reaching one behind the other up to the middle and then projecting one beyond the other, in the upper half. Above these is a palm tree capital. They are separated by a row of rosettes. The upper half of the wall is also paneled and some of the sculptured slabs are still to be seen. The figure, however, are of same crude type that is seen in most of these *baolis*. There are two panels on the outer side of the walls, each panel depicting a sculptured group showing a fully accoutered elephant driven by a mahavat fighting a lion. On other slabs there are the ubiquitous Ganesa and coiled snake[11].

4. Baoli of Dhatha Dhanda.

Six kilometers above Rajouri there is an old Hindu boli of Dhatha Dhanda which still possesses some crude sculptures one of which has a hunting scene, a fully armed horseman with sword and shield chasing a wild animal, probably a boar or a bear[12].

5. Jandi.

There are several natural springs scattered around the Jandi village. It is said that great saint Jamdagani, finding it most congenial place for meditation, meditated for years together by the side of main spring. It was named after the great saint, as Jandi, people comes here on Baisakhi and some other auspicious days to take bath in Jamdagni or Jandi kund.[13]

6. Airwan.

There are a large number of *baolies* at Airwan, about 15 kms. from Kathua district. Airwan is a holy place of Guptganga, where a big reservoir of water is fed by natural springs. It is said that Airawat, the king elephant was reborn here hence the name of the village Airwan became popular. It is supposed to be a pious place that the people who do not afford to go to Haridwar to immerse last remains of their kith and kin do so here. It is said that the number of the *baolies* more than seven hundred at the adjoining areas of Airwan. At present there is three main *baolies* in Airwan, first one is for ladies second for gents and third for kith and kins. The people, especially woman folk take bath early in the morning before offering worship in the temple. Nearby there is an ancient Shiva temple. A Bath in these springs on Baisakhi is considered very meritorious[14].

7. Mandli baoli

Mandli *baoli* is newly constructed *baoli,* in which a few old slabs bearing a coiled Naga, a Seshasyi and Bhairva have been inserted. Another important *baoli* about three miles from Thara –Kadwal and the on the way to Khun, is a large *baoli* and a set of remarkably well sculptured panels. The basin is about 15 feet square and of the usual type. The basin is enclosed on three sides within thick stone walls, receding in terraces one above the other. There are two at the sides and three behind[15]. The lower walls of the sides and the middle one at the back are plain. But the lower wall at the back has, besides the well designed lion head, two trefoil niches with projecting lotus -leaf bases and lotus leaf decoration above the Chhajja. One of these contains a figure of Ganesa and the other coiled snake.

8. Bilawar.

The township of Billawar is beautifully located on the slope of a wooden hill which has the Naj Nullah flowing at its feet. There are a large number of *baolis* around the Bilwakeswar temple area[16]. Many of them are dilapidated, but there are some which are still in good condition. One of the *baolis,* still extent is a large structure, beautifully constructed with well dressed stones. It is an enclosed edifice with a gushing spring of cool, refreshing water in the middle. The *baoli* supplies water for ablutions and for offering to the temple deity.

In fact on festival days, there are pots full of water outside the temple for devotees to sprinkle on the lingam inside. Opposite Balaur on the bank of the torrent is the village of Gurnal. In the small area of Gurnal are said to be 101 *baolis*[17].

9. Sukrala

A *baoli* at Sukral (Kathua district) has been described in detail by R.C.Kak[18]. It is a square *baoli* situated at the upper end of the village. The back wall of this structure has a number of panels in a row bearing sculptures in relief. Going from left to right them are:

1. A conventional tree, probably cypress:

2. Matsyavatara, with upper human body and the lower half that of a fish;

3. The sun, shaped like an expanded lotus with pointed petals, and moon, a circular medallion with four scan thus leaves carved on it;

4. Hanuman clad in dhoti, running;

5. A cypress tree;

6. Four armed Narasimhavatara tearing the bowels of the Asura;

7. A dead goose with its neck bent down;

8. A body in *palaki* being carried by four bearers, and a cavalier armed with sword and shield with an attendant walking behind him holding a chauri over cavalier's head (a lari-lara-relief)

9. Another cypress;

10. Four armed Durga astride a lion;

11. A lozenges; and

12. A coiled snake.

Higher up there is another *baoli* with a larger and thicker wall. On its one side is an arched takcha containing an image of Shiva and Parvati seated side by side. The Ganga flowing from Shiva's hair covers the whole body of the goddess. On the other end is the figure of the four-headed Brahma holding four Vedas in his hands. At the back side in the lower platform are two takchaas in one which is a slab bearing a bearded rider, and in the second an image of Shiva[19]. There is a more elaborately ornamented takcha above the latter, which contains a figure of Seshsayi, Visnu. At his feet is Lakshmi. From his naval springs the lotus-stalk on which Brahma is seated. On either side of Brahma are two rosettes. Another niche beside this one has a slab on which the figure of a lady is carved.

10. Mahanpur

In the area of Mahanpur (Kathua district) many small *baolis* are found but the most important is in the front of Jagdamba temple of Mahanpur. It is square type and is said to have been built by Maharaja Gulab Singh[20]. The Thakur dvara, the dharmasala and the baoli near them are said to have been built by Maharaja Gulab Singh's mother, the Rani Paddual. The *baolis* has stair type ground level to step by step down to surface of water level. As on the Dhar- Udhampur road, *baolis* on this road found at after two or three miles[21]. They are two types. The first is most common, is a natural spring whose water is enclosed in a small square stepped basin narrowing towards the base and enclosed in masonry walls on the sides and the back. Its water surface is always level with the surrounding ground. The second, probably the latter type, is a deep circular well with water far below the surface of the ground. The water level is approached by a long flight of steps leading down from the upper ground level[22]. These steps are enclosed in masonry walls. It is said that a dozen baolis of the second type were constructed in Raja Suchet Singh (1622-1643 A.D.) time, on the high road between Basholi and Mansar by one Jawahar Singh, a merchant.

11. Liran wali baoli (the spring of ribbons).

Some 12 kilometer above Rajouri towards Thanna is situated the Liran wali *baoli* (the spring of ribbons). Its right wall bears a couple of horsemen fully accoutered following each other. On its left wall is a clumsy Shivalinga. Such *baolis* are frequently met with in this tract but all of them have lost their sculptural wealth. There are number of Hindu *baolis* at Thanna and in surrounding villages[23].

References:

1. Gupta, Lalit., Commemorative Volume, Digital Publication, New   Delhi,1998.   p. 173
2. Charak, S.D.S., Anita Billawria., History and Culture of Himalayan States, Jay Kay
    Book House, Jammu, 1997,P. 115.
3. Ibid.
4. Kak, R.C, Antiquities of Basholi and Ramnagar. Sagar publication, New Delhi,
    1972.p.13
5. Ibid
6. Gupta. Lalit, op.cit.p.175.
7. Ibid.
8. Charak, S.D.S.op.cit.p.117.
9. Ibid.pp-117-118.
10. Ibid, p124.
11. Ibid. pp.121-122.
12. Ibid.p124.
13. Jearth , Ashok, Hindu Shrines of the Western Himalayas, A.L.F.A, 2001,Jammu, p.166.
14. Ibid .pp.166-167
15. Kak, R.C, op.cit.p.18
16. Ganhar, J.N, Jammu Shrines and Pilgrimages, Ganhar Publication, New Delhi. 1996.
    P.53.
17. Kak, R.C, op.cit.p.10
18. Ibid.p.15
19. Charak, S.D.S.op.cit.p.122.

20. Kak, R.C, op.cit.p.6

21. Gupta. Lalit, op.cit.pp.175-176.

22. Charak, S.D.S.op.cit.p.115.

23. Ibid.124